THE
BIG TIME

TAYLOR SWIFT

AARON FRISCH

CREATIVE ◖ EDUCATION

TAYLOR SWIFT

TABLE OF CONTENTS

MEET TAYLOR

Taylor takes a pencil and paper to a quiet spot. She spends a long time writing *lyrics*. Then she practices on her guitar. She wants her song to be perfect before she sings it in front of people.

Taylor Swift makes music called country pop. She writes songs about her life. Most of Taylor's songs are about love. She says listening to her music is like reading her *diary*.

Country pop is a style of music that combines country western and pop

TAYLOR'S CHILDHOOD

Taylor was born December 13, 1989, in Reading, Pennsylvania. She liked both writing and music from an early age. By the time she was 10, Taylor was playing guitar and writing poems and songs.

The guitar has always been Taylor's favorite instrument

READING, PENNSYLVANIA

GETTING INTO MUSIC

Taylor was sometimes bullied at school, and writing songs helped her deal with that. She started singing at music contests and talent shows. She especially liked performing country songs.

Taylor's mom Andrea helped Taylor get through tough times when she was little

The Swift family moved to Nashville, Tennessee, when Taylor was 14. People call Nashville the country music **capital** of the world. In 2006, Taylor released her first song, called "Tim McGraw."

In 2011, Taylor got to perform with country star Tim McGraw

THE BIG TIME

Two years later, Taylor's next album came out. It had songs like "Love Story," and it was a huge hit. In 2008, Taylor's albums sold 4 million copies. That was more than any other musician that year!

....

Taylor sang her hit song "Love Story" at the 2008 Country Music Awards

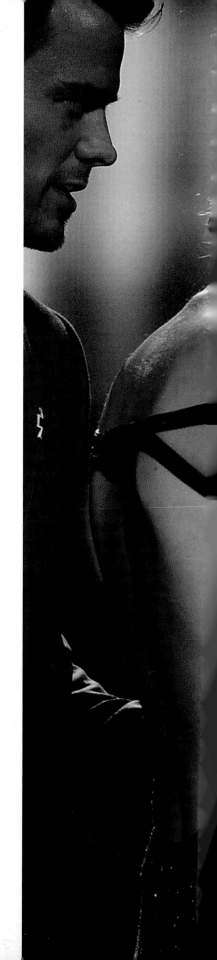

Taylor has won many honors. In 2009, she became the youngest person to win the Country Music Association award for Entertainer of the Year. Her album *Fearless* won the **Grammy Award** for 2010 Album of the Year.

....

Taylor won four Grammy Awards in 2010 and then two more in 2012

OFF THE STAGE

When she is not performing music, Taylor sometimes acts in movies and TV shows. She likes to bake foods, too. Taylor often plays concerts and then gives away the money to people who need help.

....

Taylor makes time at concerts to sign autographs

WHAT IS NEXT?

By 2012, Taylor was one of the biggest music stars in the world. And she was only 23 years old! Early in 2012, she did many concerts in Australia. She is always writing songs for her next album!

Taylor plays different kinds of guitars in her concerts and music videos

WHAT TAYLOR SAYS ABOUT ...

HER GOALS

"I am an over-achiever, and I want to be known for the good things in my life."

HER LOVE OF MUSIC

"Music is my shining light, my favorite thing in the world. To get me to stop doing it for one second would be difficult."

HER MOM

"There were times when, in middle school and junior high, I didn't have a lot of friends. But my mom was always my friend."

GLOSSARY

capital a city that is the main center for something

diary a book in which a person writes down his or her thoughts every day

Grammy Award the most famous music award in the United States

lyrics the words to a song

READ MORE

Murphy, Maggie. *Taylor Swift: Country Music Star*. New York: Powerkids, 2010.

Reusser, Kayleen. *Taylor Swift*. Hockessin, Del.: Mitchell Lane, 2011.

WEB SITES

Taylor Swift
http://www.taylorswift.com/

This is Taylor's own Web site, with news and messages from Taylor.

Taylor Swift Biography
http://www.people.com/people/taylor_swift/

This site has information about Taylor's life and many pictures, too.

INDEX

PUBLISHED BY Creative Education
P.O. Box 227, Mankato, Minnesota 56002
Creative Education is an imprint of The Creative Company
www.thecreativecompany.us

DESIGN AND PRODUCTION BY Christine Vanderbeek
ART DIRECTION BY Rita Marshall
PRINTED IN the United States of America

PHOTOGRAPHS BY Alamy (ZUMA Wire Service), Getty Images (Frederick Breedon IV/WireImage, Michael Caulfield/WireImage, Peter Kramer/NBC/NBCU Photo Bank, Scott Legato/WireImage, Sandra Mu, Kevin Winter/ACMA2011), iStockphoto (GYI NSEA, Pingebat, Cole Vineyard), Shutterstock (Featureflash, glo, s_bukley, Debby Wong)

LIBRARY OF CONGRESS CATALOGING-IN-PUBLICATION DATA
Frisch, Aaron.
Taylor Swift / Aaron Frisch.
p. cm. — (The big time)
Includes bibliographical references and index.
Summary: An elementary introduction to the life, work, and popularity of Taylor Swift, an American country and pop singer known for her versatile performances and such songs as "You Belong with Me."

ISBN 978-1-60818-333-3
1. Swift, Taylor, 1989- —Juvenile literature. 2. Country musicians—United States—Biography—Juvenile literature. 3. Women country musicians—United States—Biography—Juvenile literature. I. Title.
ML3930.S989F75 2013
782.421642092—dc23 [B]   2012013472

First edition
9 8 7 6 5 4 3 2 1